Should We Have Pets?

A Persuasive Text

Written by

Sylvia Lollis

with Joyce Hogan and her second-grade class

To Spanky—the best reason to have a pet
—S.L.

Thank you to Joyce Hogan and her wonderful second-grade authors.
An additional thank you to the school's principal, Lilly Turner, for her cooperation and support.

Photo Credits:

Front cover (large, bottom left), back cover, pp. 1 (large, bottom left), 3, 4, 5, 6 (small portraits), 8 (small portraits), 10, 12 (small portrait), 14 (small portraits), 16 (small portrait), 18 (small portraits), 20 (small portraits), 22 (small portraits), 24-30: Copyright © 2003 by Mercer Harris.

Front cover (center right), p. 14 (bottom): © Blair Seitz/Photo Researchers, Inc.; front cover (bottom right), pp. 1 (bottom right), 18 (bottom): © Fritz Prenzel/Animals Animals; p. 2: © Sylvia Lollis; p. 6 (bottom): © P. Royer/H. Armstrong Roberts, Inc.; pp. 7, 15: © Richard Hutchings/Photo Researchers, Inc.; pp. 8 (bottom), 16 (bottom): © Alfred B. Thomas/Animals Animals; pp. 9 (left), 20 (bottom): © Renee Stockdale/Animals Animals; p. 9 (right): © Barbara Strnadova/Photo Researchers, Inc.; p. 11: © Renee Lynn/Photo Researchers, Inc.; p. 12 (bottom): © Zephyr Pictures/H. Armstrong Roberts, Inc.; p. 13: © Corbis; p. 17: © John J. Dommers/Photo Researchers, Inc.; p. 19: © C.S. Bauer/H. Armstrong Roberts, Inc.; p. 21: © Gibbs, M. OSF/Animals Animals; p. 22 (bottom): © Alan Carey/Photo Researchers, Inc.; p. 23: © Robert Maier/Animals Animals.

For information contact:
MONDO Publishing, 980 Avenue of the Americas, New York, NY 10018
Visit our web site at http://www.mondopub.com

Printed in Canada
ISBN 1-59034-044-2
Designed by Jean Cohn

03 04 05 06 07 08 9 8 7 6 5 4 3 2 1

Library of Congress Cataloging-in-Publication Data
Lollis, Sylvia. Should we have pets?: a persuasive text / written by Sylvia Lollis with Joyce Hogan and her second-grade class. p.cm. Summary: A second-grade class presents arguments for and against pet ownership. ISBN: 1-59034-044-2 (pbk.) 1. Pets--Juvenile literature. [1. Pets. 2. Pet owners. 3. Children's writings.] I. Hogan, Joyce W., 1948- II. Title. SF416.2 .L65 2003 179'.3--dc21 2002033762

Contents

What Is a Pet?

Our dictionary says that the word *pet* means *an animal that is kept for enjoyment or as a companion.* The main reason people own pets is because they love animals. Some people keep pets to do jobs.

What Is a Persuasive Text?

This book asks the question, *Should we have pets?* Some of us answered *no.* Some of us think having pets is a good idea, so we answered *yes.*

Our book is a persuasive text. This means that each of us will explain how we feel about having pets. We will try to make you, the reader, agree with us.

We read books, web sites, and magazines to find facts supporting our feelings about having or not having pets. Read our arguments and decide how you feel.

Should We Have Pets? You Decide.

At the end of each argument, you will find a fishbowl.

If the bowl has a fish in it, the argument is FOR having pets. If the bowl is empty, the argument is AGAINST having pets. After reading each argument, write how strong you think the argument is.

3 points = strong

2 points = okay, fair

1 point = weak

After reading all of the arguments, add up the points you gave the arguments FOR having pets. Then add up the points you gave the arguments AGAINST having pets. Did we change your mind?

Good for the Animals

"Have you ever seen a dirty, homeless animal on the street? Well, we have, and that's why we think people should own pets—because it's good for animals."

—AMANDA ABEL AND ELIZABETH DUNAWAY

Animals need food, water, and a place to live. Pet owners give their animals these things. Too many animals starve to death or die because they don't have a home.

Pet owners take care of their animals. People feed pets, love them, and take them to the vet when they are sick.

The vet is giving the cat a checkup.

Being kept as pets is good for animals. Vote YES to having pets.

Animal Abuse

"We've seen dogs that have been left at the side of the road by their owners. Some people are mean to their pets. This is why we do not think people should own pets."

—Franklin Sherman and Roshanda Harris

Some pet owners hurt their pets. They hit or kick them. Some decide that they don't want a pet anymore and leave the animal outside without food, water, or a place to live. Some pet owners put their animals in cages that are too small.

Too many puppies are crowded together in this cage.

Being a pet can be a terrible life for an animal. This is why we do not think people should own pets. Vote NO to owning pets.

This cage is too small for the dog.

This stray dog sleeps on the street.

Pets Are Fun

"Pets are loyal, loving friends and they make their owners happy."
—BLANE WILLIAMSON AND ORIN FUSSELL

People say a dog is man's best friend but cats, birds, hamsters, and even fish make great friends, too! A pet is a great friend because it is cute, lovable, and fun to play with.

A pet that is loved and taken care of will love its owner back. Even a pet that you can't run around and play with is fun to watch and take care of.

Any pet can be a great best friend, so we say vote YES to owning pets.

Pets Cost Too Much

"Pet owners spend a lot of money on food for their animals, but many Americans go hungry."

—BreAunna Gladmon

Sometimes it seems like people care more about animals than people. Some Americans go hungry while most pets are fed fancy, expensive food.

These people are poor and hungry. They have to beg for food.

Most pet owners buy collars, brushes, dishes, leashes, toys, and cages for their pets, too. When a pet gets sick, the owner must pay for the vet and medicine.

This pet store sells expensive things people can buy for their pets.

I think the money pet owners spend on their animals should go to helping people instead. Vote NO to owning pets.

Pets Are Good Medicine

"When sick or elderly people are around animals, they feel less scared and lonely."

—BRITTANY PERKINS AND BILLY MCWHORTER

Pets can be great friends to everyone, but that's not all. They can also help sick children in hospitals and grown-ups in nursing homes feel better.

A woman living in a nursing home smiles as she pets a cat.

Some hospitals and nursing homes have dogs and cats come to visit. Playing with these animals makes the hospital less scary for young children. Cuddling and holding a puppy or kitten can make an older person in a nursing home smile.

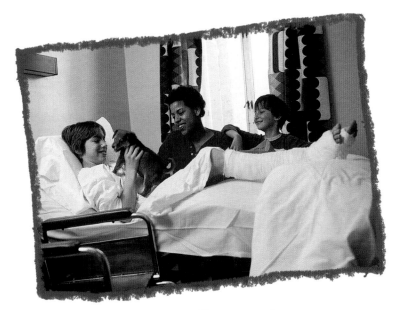

Playing with a puppy cheers up a boy in the hospital.

Pets are great friends, and they can also help sick people feel better. That's why we vote YES to having pets.

Over-breeding

"When breeders get greedy and don't care about their animals, the pets suffer."
—MICKEY REVILLE

Each year thousands of puppies come from puppy mills, where owners over-breed dogs for one reason—money! They over-breed dogs and other animals hoping to sell them all.

These puppies are crowded into a small cage at a puppy mill.

Over-bred animals often have problems. Some are blind or deaf. Some have bad hearts, hip problems, or brain damage. Many of these sick animals are abandoned and left to die. Some breeders take sick dogs to animal shelters or put them to sleep.

These extra puppies were left at an animal shelter.

If people weren't willing to buy pets, breeders wouldn't over-breed them. For this reason, I vote NO to people keeping pets.

Working Pets

"Animals have been trained to help people do jobs for hundreds of years."

—Dexter Rouse, Shantel Elam, and Pierra Heath

Some animals that are kept as pets also work. Dogs can be trained to herd sheep, guard homes, find bombs, pull sleds, catch mice, and help blind people get around.

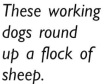
These working dogs round up a flock of sheep.

Horses that work by carrying or pulling loads are often thought of as pets by their owners. Pet birds can be trained to deliver important messages.

These horses pull a load of logs out of the forest.

We think that pets are great helpers. If you agree, you should vote YES for pets.

Animals Should Be Free

"Pet birds have a small space to walk in but not enough room to fly. Some birds get so bored, they pull their own feathers out."

—ROSHANDA HARRIS AND FRANKLIN SHERMAN

We think animals should be free. Animals kept as pets aren't free. It's cruel to keep dogs, cats, birds, fish, rabbits, or any other animals indoors, in cages, or away from their natural habitats.

Most dogs and cats are kept indoors. Most wild dogs roam in packs, and pet dogs would act this way, too, if they were free. Cats are natural hunters that prowl around hunting when given the chance.

Birds are meant to fly, but most pet birds are kept in tiny cages. Fish should be free to swim in ponds, lakes, or oceans, but most pet fish are kept in small bowls or tanks. Living in a cage or bowl your whole life would be very lonely.

Animals should be free, not kept as pets. We vote NO to owning pets.

We Can Learn From Pets

"Our pets have taught us a lot."

—BLANE WILLIAMSON AND ORIN FUSSELL

Owning a pet is hard work. A pet owner must remember to feed and clean the animal and to bring it to the vet for checkups. Owning a pet teaches a person responsibility, which is an important quality.

a mother hamster and babies

Having a pet is also educational. Pet owners learn what different animals eat, when they sleep, and how they act. They might even get to see their pet have babies. Owning a pet is a science lesson every day.

Taking care of a pet teaches responsibility and it's educational. We vote YES to owning pets.

Cast Your Vote

You have read our arguments for having pets.

Amanda Abel

Elizabeth Dunaway

Blane Williamson

Orin Fussell

Brittany Perkins

Billy McWhorter

Dexter Rouse

Shantel Elam

Pierra Heath

You have read our arguments against having pets.

Franklin Sherman

Roshanda Harris

BreAunna Gladmon

Mickey Reville

Now add up your points and cast your vote. Are you FOR or AGAINST having pets?

How We Wrote
Our Persuasive Book

Our class loves animals. About half of us own pets. None of us had ever thought about the question, *Should we have pets?* At first, we all answered YES. But some of us changed our minds as we learned more.

We enjoyed writing this book. Here's how we did it:

1. We read as much as we could on the subject.

2. We brainstormed what we thought about pets. Then we wrote down our thoughts in two columns, FOR and AGAINST.

3. We grouped similar arguments under larger headings.

4. Each of us chose the one argument we liked best—
FOR or AGAINST having pets.

5. We formed groups with other students who agreed
with us.

6. We wrote the main idea that supported our argument.

7. We added details to support our main idea. These
were our first drafts.

8. We edited our own writing and then worked in pairs
to edit each other's work.

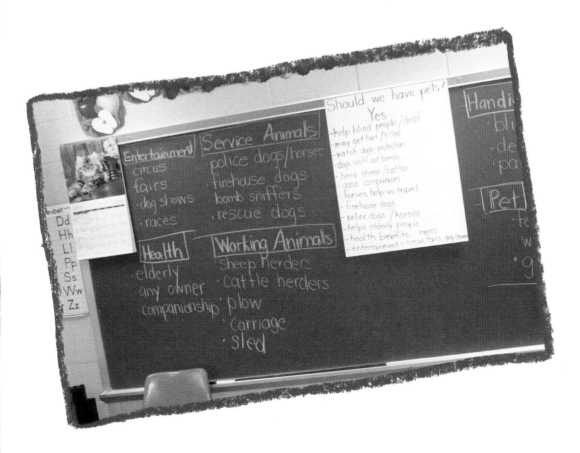

9. Our teachers helped us revise and edit one final time.

10. We brought our pets to school. Mr. Harris, the photographer, took photos of each student with his or her pet.

11. Finally, we published our arguments using our best handwriting or a classroom computer.

Glossary

abandon to leave or give up

abuse to treat in a harmful way

animal breeder a person who brings animals together so they will have babies

argument something spoken or written that is meant to convince others of a point of view

companion a friend

deliver to bring something to another place or person

enjoyment	fun
habitat	the place an animal lives in nature
homeless	being without a house or other place to live
loyal	remaining someone's friend forever
over-breed	to force animals to have more babies than is healthy
responsibility	a job or act that a person has promised to do
support	to be in favor of

Index

A

abandon, 17
abuse, 8
animal breeder, 16, 17
animal shelter, 17
argument, 4, 5, 24, 25, 27, 28

B

bird, 10, 19-21

C

cages, 8, 13, 20, 21
cat, 10, 15, 20, 21
companion, 4

D

death, 6, 17
dog, 8, 10, 15-18, 20, 21

E

education, 23
elderly, 14
enjoyment, 4

F

fish, 10, 20, 21
fishbowl, 5, 21
food, 6, 8, 12
friend, 10, 11, 14, 15
fun, 10, 11

H

habitat, 20
hamster, 10
homeless, 6
horse, 19
hospital, 14, 15
hungry, 12

J

job, 4, 18

K

kitten, 15